SILVER HAYZZ

Self-Healing for Beginners

The First Steps to Better Health

First edition

This book was professionally typeset on Reedsy.
Find out more at reedsy.com

Contents

Introduction

Have you ever felt like you're running on empty, giving all your energy to others while barely saving any for yourself? You're not alone. Many of us find ourselves caught in this cycle, wondering how to break free and regain our balance. That's where self-healing comes in. It's not just a buzzword; it's a lifeline.

Welcome to "Self-Healing for Beginners: The First Steps to Better Health." This book is your guide to understanding basic energy healing. It's designed for those who are curious about energy healing but don't know where to start.

As a trained Reiki practitioner, I've spent years learning how to help others. But let me tell you, it's a whole different ball game when it comes to taking care of myself. I've struggled with putting my own health first, both mentally and physically. Even after my Reiki attunements, I often found myself prioritizing others' needs over my own. This book is as much a reminder to myself as it is an encouragement to you.

Self-healing is about more than just fixing what's broken. It's about empowering yourself to live a fuller life. In a world that's constantly demanding more from us, self-healing offers a way to recharge and find peace. It's accessible, and it's something you can integrate into your daily life without needing special equipment or tons of free time.

Let's talk about the benefits. You'll discover ways to reduce stress, adopt healthier lifestyle habits, and protect your well-being. These practices are not just about surviving; they're about thriving. When you feel good, everything else in life becomes a little easier to manage.

This book outlines a seven-day framework filled with exercises and practices. Each day, you'll learn a new aspect of energy healing. You'll find practical steps to incorporate these techniques into your life. It's tailored for beginners, so no prior experience is necessary.

Whether you're a complete novice or someone looking to deepen your understanding, you'll find useful insights here. The focus is practical and down-to-earth, making it easy to apply what you learn.

Throughout this journey, you'll gain a better understanding of yourself and your needs. You'll face challenges, but don't worry. We'll talk about how to overcome them. Think of this book as both a map and a friend, guiding you to a healthier, more balanced life.

I want to encourage you to commit to your own well-being. Self-care isn't selfish; it's necessary. I've been there, caught up in the whirlwind of life, forgetting to care for myself. This book is my way of reminding both you and me to take that step back and focus on what truly matters.

So, are you ready to start your self-healing journey? Dive in with an open mind and a heart ready for growth. Let's take these first steps together. The path to better health starts now.

1

Chapter 1: Laying the Foundation for Self-Healing

E ver find yourself swamped with tasks and forget to schedule "me time"? Balancing life's demands while maintaining your well-being often feels like juggling flaming torches—exciting yet daunting. This chapter is your first step toward reclaiming balance and prioritizing yourself.

Understanding Self-Healing: A Beginner's Guide

Self-healing taps into your innate ability to foster health and well-being, essential in our fast-paced lives. Historically, cultures worldwide have embraced it, from ancient Chinese medicine to indigenous rituals, emphasizing that healing nurtures the whole self, not just symptoms. Dry throats, snotty noses, headaches and tummy issues are the worst, but they aren't the root cause.

The holistic nature of self-healing integrates mind, body, and spirit, transforming your perspective like upgrading from black-and-white to HD colour. This approach aligns with holistic health practices that emphasize balance and harmony.

Self-healing shines in personal empowerment, fostering self-awareness and enabling you to take charge of your health. It's liberating, though slightly daunting, to know you're responsible for your well-being.

Let me say that again, **YOU ARE RESPONSIBLE FOR YOUR WELL-BEING!** We can't rely on others to do it for us because it is our lives to live.

The benefits of taking action can range from reduced stress to healthier habits, despite inevitable challenges. Consider these challenges as essential plot twists in your personal growth story.

Demystifying Energy: Chakras, Meridians, and Auras

Energy in healing? Picture it as the body's Wi-Fi, connecting everything seamlessly. This invisible force keeps us balanced. In holistic health, energy is life's fuel, maintaining harmony.

Chakras, the body's energy hubs, influence both physical and emotional health. Imagine them as spinning wheels along your spine, each with its own mission—from grounding your roots to inspiring creativity. When chakras are balanced, life flows smoothly; when blocked, chaos ensues.

Meridians, on the other hand, are like highways for energy flow, routing vitality to every nook and cranny. Traditional Chinese medicine views these pathways as crucial for maintaining balance and health. Acupuncture targets these paths, offering relief by unblocking stuck energy.

Then there's the aura, your personal energy shield interacting with the world. It has layers that reflect your inner state. Keeping it clean is like dusting off cobwebs—necessary for clarity. Techniques for cleansing include visualizations or simply spending time in nature.

The Mind-Body Connection: How Thoughts Affect Health

Psychoneuroimmunology, or PNI if you prefer a tongue twister, explores how our mind influences our body; it is the study of how the immune and central nervous systems interact. Ever notice a headache when you're stressed? That's your body talking. Research shows stress affects immune function, making us more susceptible to illness (Psychoneuroimmunology: The Mind-Body Connection). Emotions like anger, anxiety, or sadness can manifest as physical symptoms—think of stress-induced ulcers or chronic back pain. Positive thinking, though, can work wonders. Optimism isn't just a mood booster; it aids recovery and improves health outcomes. Techniques like gratitude journaling and affirmations can cultivate positivity (Gratitude Journaling and Mental Health). Practicing mindfulness—being present—helps reduce stress and strengthens the mind-body link. Mindfulness meditation is an effective tool for this. So, next time you feel overwhelmed, take a moment to breathe and be present.

Common Misconceptions About Energy Healing

Energy healing is often misunderstood, shrouded in myths like it's some mystical, unproven practice. One might think it's only for the spiritually inclined or that it can cure anything. Let's bust these myths.

Energy healing focuses on balance, not miracles. It's a complement, not a replacement for medical treatments. Scientific studies back this, showing energy's impact on stress and emotional health (Energy Medicine: Current Status and Future Perspectives).

Let's consider logical reasoning and real-life success stories. Picture someone overcoming chronic stress through Reiki sessions—transformative, right? Personal experiences reveal energy healing's subtle power. Explore with open minds, embracing new possibilities without expecting instant magic.

Setting Intentions for Your Healing

Setting intentions is giving your energy a GPS—clear directions for your healing journey. Begin by asking yourself what you truly want to achieve. Write it down. Be specific. A well-crafted intention turns vague dreams into actionable goals. Think of it as planting a seed; with care and focus, it grows.

Intentions shape outcomes by directing energy, creating a pathway for healing. When you set an intention, you initiate change rather than just hoping for it. This is a powerful statement, and I have several sheets of paper around the house with it written on to remind me:

Intention = Power

Not, "I intend to do..." because we all know it never gets done. Instead, use "By doing this, my intention is..." because our actions are set in the intention.

Visualize your intention daily. Picture it vividly, as if it's already happening. Journaling clarifies what matters, offering a safe space to refine thoughts.

Reflect regularly and adjust intentions as needed. Life evolves, and so should your goals. Track progress, celebrating small victories. This practice keeps you aligned, fostering growth and transformation.

Setting intentions is more than a task—it's a commitment to self-care and personal evolution. Embrace this process, allowing your intentions to guide you towards a vibrant, purposeful existence.

2

Chapter 2: Practical Techniques for Daily Stress Reduction

Breathing Exercises for Instant Calm
Notice how stress turns your breathing shallow and rushed? Your breath, when controlled, is a potent stress reliever. Diaphragmatic, or belly breathing, enhances oxygen intake and soothes the nervous system, dropping heart rates and blood pressure for a quick calm.

Try the 4-7-8 method: inhale through the nose for four counts, hold for seven, and exhale audibly through the mouth for eight.

Or use box breathing: inhale for four, hold for four, exhale for four, and hold for another four. These techniques effectively reset the mind. Integrate breath awareness into daily tasks, like waiting in line or doing dishes, to consciously focus on breathing.

Exercise: Breathing Routine Checklist

- **Morning wake-up**: Begin with three minutes of deep breathing.
- **Afternoon reset**: Apply the 4-7-8 method during lunch breaks.
- **Evening wind-down**: End the day with box breathing before sleep.

Guided Visualization: Creating Your Safe Space

Imagine closing your eyes and stepping into a world where stress vanishes, replaced by calm and clarity. That's the power of guided visualization, a technique that taps into your imagination to reduce stress. By conjuring mental images, you create a sanctuary in your mind where worries can't intrude. Visualization helps clear mental clutter, enhancing focus like a mental tidy-up.

To craft your personal sanctuary, think of a place where you feel utterly at peace. Maybe it's a beach where the waves whisper secrets. Add sensory details—like the scent of saltwater or the warmth of the sun on your skin—to make it vivid. Visualization isn't just daydreaming; it's a tool for mental clarity. It helps you de-clutter thoughts and sharpen concentration.

Enhance these experiences by using guided audio recordings or weaving them into meditation. These tools deepen the experience, making it richer and more engaging. Your mind deserves a vacation, and guided visualization provides the perfect getaway.

Progressive Muscle Relaxation Techniques

Progressive Muscle Relaxation (PMR) is akin to giving your body a spa day at home. Conceived by Dr. Edmund Jacobson in the 1920s, it emphasizes tension and release in each muscle group to alleviate stress, proving that a calm body fosters a relaxed mind. Stress often pairs with tight muscles, creating an unwelcome combination.

For PMR, begin with your toes, tensing them briefly before releasing. Progress upwards to your calves, thighs, up to your face, ensuring to breathe deeply throughout. This technique can alleviate headaches and muscle pains and improve sleep quality, shifting from restless nights to restful slumbers. Incorporate PMR into your routine, perhaps before bed, as it offers not just muscular relaxation but also mental unwinding from life's stresses.

Quick Mindfulness Practices for Busy Lives

Mindfulness sounds fancy, but it's just about being present. Imagine noticing the world around you instead of rushing through life. It's like savouring a piece of chocolate instead of gobbling it down. Mindfulness shrinks stress by helping you pause and breathe.

A five-minute body scan is a quick fix—close your eyes, focus on each body part, and let tension melt away. Mindful eating is fun too; notice flavours and textures as you chew. The beauty of mindfulness lies in its adaptability; practice during commutes or while chatting with friends. Shift your mindset to stay present. Little reminders, like sticky notes or phone alerts, can nudge you back to the now.

Gratitude Journaling for Stress Relief

Gratitude journaling is like capturing sunshine in a jar—it's simple yet transformative. By jotting down what you're thankful for, you shift your focus from what's wrong to what's right, making the glass seem half full, not half empty. Research shows that this practice can boost your mood, reducing feelings of depression by highlighting the positive aspects you often overlook (Gratitude Journaling and Mental Health).

Start by picking a journal format that suits you; whether it's a fancy notebook or an app, choose what feels right. Use prompts like "What made me smile today?" or "Who are the people I'm grateful for?" to guide your entries. Consistency is key, so set aside time daily, perhaps pairing it with your evening routine to end the day on a positive note.

In wrapping up this chapter, remember that small practices can have significant impacts. Each technique offers a step toward a calmer mind. Up next, we explore how to manifest healing through energy work, deepening your self-care toolkit even further.

3

Chapter 3: Exploring Energy Systems: Techniques and Applications

Basic Chakra Balancing Techniques
Chakras, the body's energy centres, can be likened to gears in an engine; when aligned, life flows smoothly. The seven main chakras begin with the Root Chakra at the spine's base, essential for grounding, and extend to the Crown Chakra, connecting to universal consciousness (Balancing Chakras: Techniques & Practices, 2023).

Balancing chakras might resemble tuning an instrument. Visualization can be a helpful tool: imagine a red light at the Root Chakra spinning freely and adjust each chakra as you move upwards.

Personally, I imagine each Chakra being a flower of its represented colour, slightly open with vibrant petals. If any of the petals are wilting or damaged, then I know more work is needed in this area.

Affirmations further support this practice, such as "I am grounded" for the Root and "I express myself easily" for the Throat Chakra.

Crystals and essential oils offer additional support—rose quartz can enhance the Heart Chakra, while lavender oil benefits the Crown. Regular meditation and check-ins ensure chakras remain aligned, fostering balanced well-being and harmony.

Understanding and Using Meridians in Daily Life

Think of meridians as invisible highways that transport energy throughout your body, keeping everything in sync. These pathways—rooted in ancient practices—help maintain balance, much like how water flows through a riverbed to nourish the land. The major meridians include lines like the lung, heart, and kidney meridians, each associated with specific organs and functions. Acupuncture taps into these lines, using tiny needles to stimulate energy flow and restore harmony.

To keep your energy flowing, try tapping along these meridian lines. Start with gentle taps from head to toe, focusing on areas like the collarbone and wrist. Stretching exercises targeting meridian pathways can also be invigorating. Acupressure offers quick relief for common issues: pressing the point between your thumb and index finger can ease headaches, while a spot just below the kneecap helps with stress.

Incorporate these practices into your daily life by focusing on breathing exercises that activate meridians. Try tapping along these lines during your morning routine to set a positive tone for the day.

Grounding Practices to Center Your Energy

Grounding is like recharging your internal battery by connecting with the earth. Simple grounding exercises can work wonders. Try walking barefoot on natural surfaces—sand, grass, soil—and notice how it centres you. This process isn't just physical; it anchors your emotions, offering clarity.

Visualization is another powerful tool; Imagine standing barefoot on cool grass, feeling every blade underfoot and letting the earth's energy stabilize your own. Imagine roots growing from your feet, anchoring you to the earth. Roots extending deep into the soil, drawing strength and balance from the ground.

When life's whirlwind spins you around, grounding restores calm and focus, reducing anxiety and overwhelm. Regular grounding practices enhance physical health, alleviating stress and improving sleep by promoting relaxation.

Incorporate grounding into daily life with morning rituals; sip your coffee outside, feel the sun on your skin, and breathe deeply. Or garden mindfully, connecting with nature as you tend to plants. These simple habits create a strong foundation for emotional stability and mental clarity.

Simple Aura Cleansing Methods

Think of your aura as your own personal force field, an energy cocoon reflecting your inner state. This invisible shield has layers, like an onion (not an Ogre), each serving a unique purpose. The outermost guards against negativity, while the inner layers mirror emotions and health. When your aura is vibrant, you feel energized and positive. But when cluttered, it can drag you down.

Start by cleansing with simple techniques like smudging. Burn sage or incense; let the smoke waft around you, removing negativity like a cosmic dust buster. Sound vibrations also work wonders—chanting or using singing bowls can cleanse your aura.

Keeping your aura clear boosts your mood and energy. It acts as a protective bubble, keeping out the bad vibes and inviting in the good ones. For regular maintenance, scan your aura for blockages by sensing changes in temperature or tingling sensations. Visualize healing light repairing any tears. These habits ensure your energy stays aligned and your interactions remain positive.

Integrating Energy Work into Routine Activities

Consistency in energy work is like watering a plant; it nurtures steady growth. Daily energy check-ins, like a quick mental scan during your morning coffee, keep you in tune with your needs. Energy rituals can fit snugly into your schedule, like a puzzle piece finding its place. Consider energy clearing during your daily shower—imagine the water washing away negativity, leaving you refreshed.

Infusing meals with positive energy adds a pinch of mindfulness to cooking. Stir with intention, and let gratitude be your secret ingredient. Mindful awareness in energy practices makes each moment count. Before starting, set clear intentions and cultivate presence. This focus transforms ordinary actions into powerful energy work.

Personalize routines to reflect your style. Develop an energy toolkit tailored to you; perhaps crystals meet yoga mats. Blend energy work with hobbies, like meditative knitting or energizing dance. As we wrap up, remember this integration enhances well-being, ready to support your journey into deeper practices in the next chapter.

4

Chapter 4: Emotional and Mental Healing Practices

Emotional Release Techniques: Letting Go of What No Longer Serves You
Holding onto negative emotions can feel like a packed traffic jam—it's exhausting and hinders progress. Releasing these emotions is crucial for healing, allowing you to unload the burden and move forward freely. Stagnant emotions can impact physical health, causing stress and discomfort. The connection between emotional and physical well-being is intertwined and essential.

Expressive journaling offers a way to release emotions. Write uncensored thoughts, letting them flow freely. Emotional Freedom Techniques (EFT) involve tapping specific body points while focusing on emotions, akin to acupuncture minus needles.

Forgiveness is vital in emotional release. It's not about condoning past actions but liberating oneself from them. Personal forgiveness exercises and guided meditations are tools to help untie emotional knots.

Reflection Section: Forgiveness Meditation Guide

- Find a quiet, comfortable space.
- Close your eyes and take deep breaths.

- Visualize someone or something you need to forgive.
- Silently say, "I release you and set myself free."
- Picture the weight lifting from your heart as your body becomes lighter and more freeing.

Creating a safe space for emotional expression is essential. Design a personal sanctuary, perhaps a cozy nook with gentle lighting. Set boundaries for emotional self-care, ensuring interruption-free time to explore your feelings. This space becomes a refuge to safely process and release emotions.

Building Emotional Resilience: Tools for Life's Challenges

Emotional resilience is like your mental armour, helping you bounce back when life throws curveballs. Picture it as your inner superhero cape. Those with this superpower handle stress better and adapt quickly. They see setbacks as challenges rather than insurmountable walls. It's all about weathering storms without losing your cool. The benefits are clear: less stress, better relationships, and a more positive outlook.

To bolster your resilience, try stress inoculation training. Think of it as a mental boot camp, preparing you for tough times with controlled exposure to stressors, boosting your coping skills. Create a resilience-boosting routine by incorporating activities like mindfulness or yoga. Surround yourself with a network of supportive relationships, like a safety net of understanding and encouragement. Consider joining resilience-focused support groups where shared experiences build strength.

Regularly practice gratitude; it's like a magic potion for resilience. Engage in creative expression—paint, write, dance—as it fortifies emotional strength. Life's challenges become manageable hurdles with these tools in your kit.

Cognitive Exercises for Mental Clarity

Mental clarity is like having a GPS for your thoughts, guiding you through life's chaos. It sharpens decision-making and reduces stress. When your mind is cluttered, it's like trying to find a pen in a junk drawer—frustrating and time-consuming. But worry not! Mind mapping can help you sort through complex problems visually, making it easier to see connections and solutions. For a fun twist, try brain-training games or puzzles; they're like a workout for your brain, keeping it fit and agile.

Your diet also plays a role in mental sharpness. Foods rich in omega-3s, like salmon and walnuts, boost brain health. Staying hydrated is crucial too; even slight dehydration can fog your mind. To keep mental clutter at bay, consider a digital detox. Set aside time to unplug from screens, giving your brain a break. Establish a mental de-cluttering routine, perhaps starting with five minutes of quiet reflection each day. A clear mind not only enhances self-healing but also makes daily life feel less overwhelming and more manageable.

The Power of Affirmations in Healing

Imagine affirmations as the little pep talks you give your brain. They work wonders by rewiring those neural pathways, reinforcing positive beliefs. Think of it like training a puppy; consistent reinforcement shapes behaviour. So, when you say, "I am strong," your mind starts believing it, nudging you toward strength. Affirmations act as positive reinforcement, shifting self-perception and boosting confidence.

Crafting effective affirmations is an art. Always use the present tense—"I am calm" rather than "I will be calm." Tailor them to specific goals, making them personal and direct. You might say, "I embrace my creativity" if that's your focus.

Incorporate affirmations into your daily routine seamlessly. Begin with morning rituals; while sipping your coffee, repeat your affirmations aloud or silently. Use apps designed to prompt you with reminders throughout the day. Consistency is key; the more you repeat them, the stronger their impact. Create visual affirmation boards, plastered with inspiring words and images, serving as constant reminders of your intentions.

Introspection and Self-Reflection: A Path to Emotional Intelligence

Introspection is like holding up a mirror to your soul, enhancing understanding of your thoughts and emotions. It's vital for developing emotional intelligence—the ability to recognize, understand, and manage emotions.

This self-awareness fosters healthier relationships since you're more attuned to your feelings and those of others. Emotional intelligence extends beyond friendship; it's a tool for self-healing.

To practice introspection, try reflective journaling with prompts to deeply explore feelings. Mindful meditation boosts self-awareness, helping you observe thoughts without judgment.

Emotional intelligence aids in stress management. By recognizing emotional triggers, you can respond more calmly in stressful situations. It enhances empathy, fostering deeper connections with others.

Make self-reflection a habit. Allocate weekly time for introspection and create a toolkit that inspires thoughtfulness. Embrace this practice as part of your self-healing journey.

Understanding yourself unlocks potential. As we proceed, let's explore how physical health complements emotional well-being in the next chapter.

5

Chapter 5: Creating a Personalized Self-Healing Plan

Assessing Your Personal Healing Needs

Have you ever felt like a cookie-cutter solution just doesn't work for your unique self? Understanding your healing needs is vital to creating a tailored self-healing plan, much like designing a custom suit. Begin with a self-assessment inventory by honestly examining your life to identify areas that feel off. Is stress an unwelcome visitor? Are sleep and nutrition elusive? It's time to personalize your approach.

Start by compiling a personal health history, noting significant events affecting wellness, such as job-related stress or diet patterns. Evaluate your current lifestyle: Are you couch-bound more than desired, or is your diet disorderly? Detect patterns that either aid or hinder your health goals. Trusting gut instincts can be insightful—sometimes more telling than logic. Be mindful of bodily cues and emotional signs; if something feels wrong, there's likely a reason.

Exercise: Intuitive Journaling Prompt

- Sit comfortably, close your eyes, and breathe deeply.
- Ask, "What does my body need right now?"
- Note any thoughts or feelings that emerge without judgment.

During this process, use resources like health questionnaires or online self-assessment platforms to gain clarity on your needs (Self Assessment Tools | Mandel Wellness Pathway). These tools offer insight into your current status and highlight areas needing attention.

Setting Achievable Healing Goals

Setting realistic goals is like having a road map—helpful and motivating. Think of goals as stepping stones across a stream, guiding you steadily across. Using the SMART criteria can keep you on track: Specific, Measurable, Achievable, Relevant, and Time-bound. It's like crafting a recipe, each ingredient adding value to your healing dish. Instead of saying, "I want to be healthier," try "I'll meditate for ten minutes every morning."

Breaking big goals into bite-sized pieces makes them less daunting. Create a goal hierarchy, where you start with small wins and build up to larger achievements. Imagine it as leveling up in a game, each completed task unlocking the next challenge. Weekly reviews help adjust your game plan, while monthly check-ins give perspective on your progress.

Obstacles will pop up, like pesky weeds in a garden. Identify potential roadblocks and develop contingency plans to tackle them. This way, you're prepared and not caught off guard. Balance short-term milestones with long-term visions; it's like mixing sprints with a marathon. Use vision boards to visualize success, keeping the bigger picture in sight. Celebrate small victories and keep moving forward, one step at a time!

Crafting Your Daily Self-Healing Routine

A consistent routine provides stability and propels your progress - it's like building your own sanctuary. Think of it as constructing a foundation; each daily practice aligns with your natural rhythms, grounding and guiding you. Having a structured routine doesn't mean rigid schedules. Life throws curveballs, so flexibility is key.

Picture a morning template where you meditate with a warm cup of tea, easing into the day. Or an evening wind-down with gentle yoga, stretching out the day's stress. But things change, right? Suppose it rains on your planned outdoor session, or a surprise meeting pops up. Adapt by having backup indoor activities or a shorter practice ready to go.

Variety keeps things lively and engaging. Rotate through different practices like mindfulness one day and tai chi the next, ensuring your routine stays fresh. Schedule theme days—maybe Mondays for meditation, Tuesdays for creative expression. Mix in activities like painting or writing to let emotions flow. Your daily plan might include a mindfulness session at dawn, invigorating tai chi after lunch, and some creative outlet to wrap up the day. This diversity keeps you motivated and invested in your self-healing journey.

Tracking Progress and Celebrating Milestones

Tracking your progress is like having a compass; it keeps you motivated and offers insights into your healing adventure. Accountability is key here, turning intentions into actions. As you monitor progress, use it as a reflection tool—think of it as checking your map to see how far you've come. Keeping a healing journal helps document this journey, capturing those 'aha' moments and setbacks. For the tech-savvy, digital tools and apps can track wellness metrics, offering neat graphs and reminders.

Celebrating milestones isn't just about throwing a party; it's reinforcing positive behaviour. Plan small rewards for hitting goals, whether it's a favourite treat or a break from routine. Reflect on growth and lessons learned; it builds resilience and confidence. Regularly revisit and refine goals, keeping them aligned with your evolving needs. Embrace change as your guide, adapting plans as needed.

As we wrap up this chapter, remember, tracking progress is like writing your own success story. This sets the stage for the next chapter, where we dive into deepening your energy healing practices and exploring how they integrate into everyday life. Let's keep moving forward!

6

Chapter 6: Overcoming Scepticism and Building Confidence in Energy Work

ddressing Scepticism: Evidence and Anecdotes

A Ever encountered scepticism when discussing energy work? It's common. Many see energy healing as mystical or elusive compared to conventional medicine. Questions like "Where's the proof?" or "Why don't results appear immediately?" are frequent. Let's address these with evidence and personal stories.

Scientific studies demonstrate energy work's potential. For example, research on Reiki indicates benefits beyond placebo, enhancing well-being (Reiki Is Better Than Placebo and Has Broad Potential ..., 2023). Similarly, meditation has a well-documented impact on stress reduction and mental peace (Mindfulness Meditation Is Related to Long-Lasting ..., 2023). However, personal experiences often resonate more. Many practitioners, former sceptics included, share how energy healing has changed their lives, like overcoming stress with Reiki or finding clarity through meditation. Such stories inspire hope and demonstrate possible change.

Reflection Section: Engaging with Sceptics

- Approach with curiosity, not confrontation.
- Share personal experiences without preaching.

- Invite open-ended questions to foster understanding.

In discussions, maintain an open mind. Encourage questions and explore together. Everyone's journey is personal; one method may not work for all.

Understanding the Science Behind Energy Healing

Science and energy healing might seem like oil and water, but they blend more than you'd think. Quantum physics, for instance, suggests everything is energy, including us. This isn't just sci-fi talk; it's about understanding how particles interact in mysterious ways, sometimes without even touching. The placebo effect is another mind-bender. It shows how belief alone can spark healing. Think of it as proof that our minds wield more power than we give them credit for.

Biologically, energy work can tinker with your body's processes. Ever wonder why a soothing Reiki session feels calming? It interacts with your nervous system, potentially dialing down stress hormones and boosting immunity. Research backs this up, showing how practices like meditation reshape the brain—thank you, neuroplasticity! Biophoton research even hints that our cells communicate through light, adding another layer to this healing puzzle.

Of course, the science isn't all tied up with a neat bow. Plenty of gaps exist. Some areas need more rigorous study. It's a growing field, ripe for exploration. So, keep an open mind and maybe even contribute your own insights to this evolving understanding of energy healing.

Building Trust in Your Intuition

Intuition is like that quiet friend who always knows the right thing to say, guiding you when logic and instinct fall short. It's your internal GPS in energy work, aligning you with what truly feels right. Unlike instinct, which is immediate and primal, or logic, which is calculated and methodical, intuition whispers softly, nudging you toward wisdom. Throughout history, healers have trusted intuition as a compass in their practices, relying on it to connect with unseen energies and deeper truths.

To sharpen this skill, start with intuitive decision-making exercises. When faced with a choice, pause and let your gut speak before analysing it. Meditation can also help. Close your eyes, breathe deeply, and listen for that inner voice. Pay attention to bodily sensations—they often signal your intuition's presence. The loud, persistent voice is not your intuition.

Trusting yourself in healing is vital. Self-doubt can cloud judgment, but through reflection and assurance, you empower yourself. Remember those moments when intuition led you right and use them as anchors in doubt. Stories abound of practitioners who relied on intuition for breakthroughs, revealing paths they never expected, like a sudden insight during a healing session or an intuitive nudge that proved invaluable.

Case Studies: Real-Life Success Stories

Energy healing is a tapestry woven with diverse threads of human experience. Take, for example, the story of a woman who alleviated chronic back pain through regular Reiki sessions. Her life transformed from being limited by discomfort to one of newfound freedom and vitality.

Or consider John who rebuilt emotional resilience after a traumatic event by embracing mindfulness and meditation. His practice became a sanctuary, allowing him to face life's challenges with a calm heart.

Then there's Sarah who navigated relentless anxiety with chakra balancing. Her journey was about personal growth, not just symptom relief. She found balance, not only in her energy centres but also in her daily life.

These stories share a common theme: consistency and openness to different modalities. Healing isn't a one-size-fits-all process; it's about finding what resonates with you and sticking with it.

By documenting your own experiences, you add another layer to this rich tapestry. Journaling helps capture your progress, while sharing in community forums fosters connection and support. As we wrap up this chapter, remember that your story matters too. In the next chapter, we'll explore deepening your practice with advanced techniques to enhance your healing journey.

7

Chapter 7: Building a Supportive Community and Network

Finding Your Tribe: Connecting with Like-Minded Individuals
Imagine entering a room of strangers and feeling an immediate sense of belonging—that's the essence of finding your tribe. Being part of a supportive community can significantly enhance your healing journey, providing emotional support through shared experiences and ensuring you're not alone. Group dynamics energize and motivate you, making goal adherence easier.

To discover your ideal community, identify groups that share your specific healing interests and values, akin to finding a perfectly fitting puzzle piece. Explore workshops or energy healing events where like-minded individuals congregate. Social media is invaluable, with numerous self-healing groups offering platforms for connection.

When connecting, approach with openness and authenticity. Share your stories; vulnerability fosters bonds. Practice active listening and empathy, appreciating every voice in the conversation. Engage with genuine curiosity and a welcoming spirit, and you'll soon find your tribe.

Reflection Section: Journaling Prompt

• What qualities do I seek in a supportive community?

- How can I contribute positively to the groups I join?

The Importance of a Supportive Environment

Creating a supportive environment is like giving your soul a warm hug. It directly impacts mental and emotional well-being, shaping how you feel day-to-day. Your physical space, believe it or not, plays a huge role in emotional health. A cluttered room can mirror a cluttered mind, while a tidy space promotes clarity. Try adding plants; they're natural stress busters, and a splash of sunlight can lift even the gloomiest mood. Your social surroundings matter too. Surrounding yourself with positive folks boosts motivation, kind of like having your own cheerleading squad.

Relationships form the backbone of a nurturing atmosphere. Building trust and open communication with loved ones makes life feel like a cozy quilt of support. Setting boundaries ensures interactions remain positive, helping you maintain sanity amidst chaos. Regularly evaluate your environment to see if it aligns with your healing goals. Conduct an environmental audit— notice what drags you down or lifts you up. Make gradual changes to enhance comfort and safety, turning your home into a sanctuary of peace.

Engaging in Online Communities for Healing

Online support networks for self-healing offer a global treasure trove of perspectives and resources. They connect you with individuals from diverse backgrounds, all sharing a common interest in energy healing. This virtual realm provides a wealth of experiences and insights that can broaden your understanding and practice. When searching for the right online community, evaluate community guidelines and values. Look for platforms with vibrant interactions where members actively engage and share. This ensures you're stepping into a space that aligns with your goals and beliefs.

Online interactions can be both a boon and a challenge. They allow for meaningful connections across miles, yet miscommunications can sometimes pop up like unexpected glitches. Stay mindful of tone and context, and you'll navigate these digital waters smoothly. To maximize your engagement, dive into discussions with genuine curiosity. Share your own experiences and insights; they add value to the community tapestry. Consider leading group activities or challenges to foster camaraderie and participation.

Creating Local Meetups and Healing Circles

Local meetups are like magic potions for connection, where the power of face-to-face interactions truly shines. There's something special about gathering in person, sharing energy, and fostering real bonds. These gatherings offer hands-on learning opportunities that online chats just can't replicate. Imagine meeting others who share your passion for healing, exchanging tips, and practicing techniques together.

To organize a successful meetup, choose a comfortable, accessible spot where everyone feels at ease. Think cozy cafes or community centres. Structure events to encourage participation, maybe with icebreakers or group activities. Healing circles take things further by creating a safe haven for sharing and support. They harness collective energy and synergy, making everyone feel uplifted. When planning meetups, embrace creativity and inclusivity. Mix in diverse healing practices to accommodate different preferences and promote respect for all attendees. This chapter shows how building a supportive network enriches your healing experience.

As we wrap up this chapter, remember that community is key in healing. Whether online or in person, connections nurture growth. Next up, we'll explore advanced energy healing techniques to add to your toolkit. Get ready to deepen your understanding and practice!

8

Chapter 8: Deepening Your Practice with Advanced Techniques

Exploring Advanced Chakra Work

Ever wondered how adjusting those energy centres can feel like tuning a finely crafted instrument? Chakras, those colourful wheels of energy, do more than spin pretty. They interact intricately, much like an orchestra playing a symphony, influencing your overall flow. When chakras work in harmony, the energy flow becomes smoother, promoting emotional and spiritual growth. However, chakra knots can form, akin to tangled wires from earphones in your pocket (unless you're a clever bean with wireless earbuds), these knots can block energy and cause various issues. They need unwinding to restore balance.

For those looking to dive deeper, Kundalini yoga offers practices that activate and align chakras in profound ways. Imagine your spine as a highway and Kundalini as the electric car zooming along it, energizing each station it passes. Advanced visualization and meditation techniques cleanse chakras, akin to refreshing a web page for clarity. This work isn't just for show; it catalyses profound personal transformation. Many find that unlocking chakra potential leads to spiritual awakenings and heightened self-awareness.

To make advanced chakra work part of your daily routine, create a weekly meditation schedule, focusing on different chakras each day. Use affirmations to reinforce balance, perhaps saying, "I am grounded" while visualizing the root chakra's red glow. Integrating these practices into your life ensures lasting benefits, like consistently watering a plant to see it flourish.

Considering Reiki: The Benefits of Reiki Sessions

Reiki, rooted in the teachings of Dr Mikao Usui, began in Japan as a means to connect with universal energy for healing. Its history is a fascinating journey from Usui's 21-day fast on Mount Kurama to the bustling practice it is today. The core principles—just for today, do not anger, do not worry, be humble, be honest in your work, and be compassionate to yourself and others—guide practitioners toward balance and harmony. These principles, like a gentle nudge, remind us to live mindfully and with intent. Over time, Reiki has evolved into various modern adaptations, yet its essence remains unchanged.

Booking my first session with a professional Reiki practitioner was incredible. I had been suffering from lower abdominal pains for years, due to stress, Irritable bowel syndrome (IBS), and a combination of other things. Doctors had helped as best they could, but they couldn't alleviate the pain. Reiki had been recommended to me by a family member.

During that first session, I was giddy. I could feel the energy moving through my body, from my toes and up through my leg. I resisted the urge to laugh as I didn't want to spoil the atmosphere. At the end, the practitioner commented on my blocking the healing process. In stopping myself from laughing, I had stopped the flow of energy instead of allowing it to flow through me. Even with this setback, I could feel amazing results and wanted to know more, hence my journey began.

Regular Reiki practice offers a treasure trove of benefits. Physically, it helps relieve pain and tension. Emotionally, it fosters a tranquil mind and emotional balance. Spiritually, it enhances intuition, guiding you like a lighthouse through foggy waters. A steady practice also reduces stress, promoting relaxation akin to floating on a serene lake.

Integrating Crystals into Your Healing Practice

Crystals have always fascinated me, holding a piece of Earth in your hand, shimmering with potential. That's the magic of healing crystals, each with its own energetic signature. Whether it's the calming influence of amethyst or the protective aura of black tourmaline, these stones vibrate at frequencies that can enhance your well-being. Selecting the right crystal is like choosing a dance partner; you want one that complements your energy. Pay attention to vibrational qualities and crystal structures, as these impact how energy flows through the crystals and into you.

Choosing crystals can be as intuitive as picking a ripe fruit. Trust your gut. When you've found your crystal, cleanse it to keep its energy fresh. Methods like moonlight baths or sage smudging do the trick. Once cleansed, charge them with intentions by holding them close to your heart and thinking about the intention you want to set, so they're ready to work their magic. Advanced techniques like crystal grids involve arranging stones in geometric patterns, amplifying their power for specific goals. Combine them with other modalities, like Reiki, for a synergistic effect.

In meditation, crystals amplify focus, turning a simple session into an enlightening experience. Lay them on chakra points during balancing sessions to deepen the effect. Crystals are versatile allies in your healing toolkit, ready to enhance every practice with their shimmering energy.

Sound Healing: Using Vibrations for Balance

Sound healing is like nature's lullaby, enveloping you in vibrations that restore balance and harmony. Imagine sound waves as gentle ripples flowing through you, realigning your energy. The science behind this is fascinating— different frequencies affect your body in unique ways, promoting healing from within. Historically, sound has been used across cultures for its soothing effects, from Tibetan singing bowls to Native American drumming.

To incorporate sound into your healing practice, try using singing bowls or tuning forks. These tools clear energy blockages, much like a sonic broom sweeping away dust. Vocal toning and chanting also work wonders for self-healing. It's like giving your vocal cords a workout, releasing tension and stress. Sound deepens meditation too, guiding you to a state of relaxation and focus. Creating a sound healing playlist can enhance daily meditation or relaxation sessions.

Personalizing your sound healing routine doesn't require an orchestra. Choose instruments that resonate with you, like a favourite song that lifts your spirits. Integrate sound into your regular wellness practices to amplify benefits.

In wrapping up this chapter, sound healing offers another dimension to energy work. As we move forward, we'll explore connecting with nature to enrich our energy practices, revealing more ways to nurture our well-being.

9

Chapter 9: Sustaining Your Healing Journey

Maintaining Consistency: Overcoming Common Obstacles
Life often feels like a juggling act, and self-healing can appear as yet another task ready to topple. Obstacles like time constraints and emotional resistance create a hamster wheel effect. Facing work, family, and lack of motivation makes prioritizing difficult. However, time management techniques can turn chaos into harmony. Mindful planning—like morning meditation—ensures self-care even on busy days.

Accountability is crucial. Pair up or join a group to share goals and celebrate achievements. Flexibility is key; adapt your routines when traveling or during busy periods. Simplify during stressful times and use habit-tracking apps or journals to maintain consistency, making progress rather than perfection the aim.

Exercise: Habit-Tracking Journal Prompt

- List three daily self-healing activities.
- Monitor your completion each week.
- Reflect and adjust based on findings.

Consistency may be challenging, but with effective strategies, maintaining your self-healing journey can be graceful and manageable.

Creating a Balanced Lifestyle: Integrating Self-Healing with Daily Life

In the whirlwind of life, balance isn't just a luxury; it's a necessity. Think of it as the secret sauce that makes healing practices truly effective. Juggling work, family, and self-care can feel like a circus act. But with a little finesse, it's possible to keep those plates spinning. Balance means looking after your body, mind, and spirit. It's about finding harmony in chaos.

Incorporate healing into daily life like slipping a new ingredient into a familiar recipe. Practice mindfulness while doing mundane chores like folding laundry—let the rhythm become your meditation. A short meditation break at work can reset your mind, making productivity soar. Choose whole foods for vitality. Think of them as fuel for this well-oiled machine you call your body. Regular physical activity isn't just about staying fit; it's about feeling alive.

Your environment plays a starring role too. A calm home space acts like an anchor in stormy seas. De-clutter to clear your mind, creating an oasis where healing can thrive. Balance doesn't just happen; it's crafted thoughtfully, like a fine wine or a well-played symphony.

Staying Motivated: The Role of Reflection and Adaptation

Motivation acts like the fuel in the engine of your self-healing process, propelling you toward growth and achievement. When you're motivated, it's easier to stick with your practices and watch those healing goals come to life. But, let's face it, staying motivated can be tough. Regular self-reflection boosts motivation, giving you a clearer picture of your emotional and spiritual progress. Journaling helps; jot down your thoughts, track changes, and notice patterns. Monthly reflection rituals, like setting aside time to celebrate wins, can reignite enthusiasm and provide a sense of accomplishment.

As you continue, adapting your practices becomes vital. Explore new techniques or healing modalities to keep things fresh. Personal needs evolve, so tweak your goals and routines accordingly. Consider stories of people who found renewed motivation by embracing change. People who shifted from yoga to tai chi and felt a revitalized connection to their body. Or others that find inspiration in a simple quote: "Change is the only constant." These tales show the power of adapting and reflecting on your path, keeping motivation alive.

Handling Setbacks: Embracing Imperfection

Setbacks are like unexpected rain on your picnic. They happen, and that's okay. In self-healing, these hiccups might look like missed practices or emotional slumps. They can hit hard, leaving you deflated. But remember, setbacks are just part of the ride. The emotional impact can be discouraging, but embracing imperfection is key. Think of setbacks as growth opportunities. Each stumble offers insight, teaching you resilience and flexibility. Practice self-compassion—be kind to yourself when things don't go as planned. Forgiveness is your friend. Building resilience helps bounce back stronger. Techniques like positive reframing and mindfulness nurture resilience, transforming challenges into stepping stones. When momentum stalls, create an action plan for recovery. Break tasks into manageable chunks and celebrate small victories. Seek support from community or mentors; their guidance anchors you.

In wrapping up, setbacks aren't the end; they're lessons in disguise, guiding you toward greater self-awareness and strength. In the next chapter, we'll explore the interconnections of energy healing and self-discovery. Life is about the journey; the destination isn't as important.

10

Chapter 10: Expanding Horizons: Beyond Personal Healing

Sharing Your Healing Journey with Others
Sharing your healing journey can inspire and connect with others, much like storytelling, by building empathy and understanding. Opening up encourages shared experiences, creating a support network. To share effectively, select the right platform—be it a blog, social media, or local meetups. Balance being vulnerable with maintaining some privacy and be ready for scepticism or negative feedback; stay grounded and let your story inspire. Consider writing articles or hosting workshops. Your journey can guide others seeking their path.

Reflection Section: Journaling Prompt

- Recall a moment when your shared experiences had a positive impact.
- Consider how you can keep sharing your journey in an authentic, empowering way.

Using Self-Healing to Enhance Relationships
Transform your relationships through personal growth with self-healing, enhancing empathy and emotional intelligence. This addition helps you understand others better, turning conflicts into opportunities for connection.

Better conflict resolution skills result in fewer arguments and deeper conversations. Incorporating healing practices into relationships isn't difficult. Try active listening and mindful communication; simple yet effective. Engaging in joint meditation or relaxation exercises can turn shared moments into bonding experiences. Exploring self-healing together with your partner strengthens your bond and fosters mutual growth. Set joint personal growth goals to support each other. Challenges like resistance or scepticism may arise but focus on balancing personal and relationship needs to address them.

Applying Self-Healing Principles in Work Environments

Incorporating self-healing practices into work can transform navigating the daily grind. Replace the mid-afternoon slump with a mindful moment, enhancing focus and reducing stress. Mindfulness breaks can recharge your brain like a power nap, providing task clarity. Emotional awareness in teamwork turns colleagues into allies, fostering collaboration instead of competition. Encouraging open communication creates an atmosphere where everyone feels heard and valued. Start small by proposing brief meditations during meetings or suggesting wellness programs with stress management workshops. These initiatives promote a balanced work-life culture, leading to happier, more productive employees.

Teaching Self-Healing: Becoming a Guide for Others

Teaching self-healing is transformative, fostering a community where growth and healing thrive. It's about more than passing information; it's about enhancing well-being and mutual benefit. To be effective, develop clear workshop goals and hone communication and presentation skills. Teaching offers rewards such as personal growth and deepened understanding but also requires flexibility to manage diverse learner needs. Look for teaching opportunities both locally and online, such as hosting community events or webinars. Your insights may inspire others to begin their healing journey.

The Ripple Effect: How Personal Healing Contributes to a Better

World

Much like tossing a pebble into a pond—the ripple starts small but expands outward, influencing the entire surface. This exemplifies personal healing. As you heal, subtle changes occur in your circle, inspiring conversations with friends and family. Your growth becomes a beacon, sparking a chain of positive change. Personal transformation can inspire community initiatives or broader societal shifts, like a community garden born from a newfound love for mindfulness and sustainability. Engaging in community service or advocating for health policies can amplify this effect, fostering collective healing.

Exploring New Modalities: Keeping Your Practice Fresh

Infusing new modalities into your healing practice is like adding fresh spices to a dish, enhancing and enlivening the experience. Exploring diverse healing methods opens vast possibilities, offering fresh perspectives and preventing stagnation. Consider attending workshops or retreats for practical learning, or delve into books and articles for insights on alternative methods. While scepticisms might arise, embracing uncertainty can spark unexpected growth. It's essential to balance new practices with your routine to evolve without becoming overwhelmed.

The Role of Technology in Modern Self-Healing

Technology has revolutionized self-healing, making resources accessible at your fingertips. Imagine an app guiding you through meditation while you sip your morning coffee. Digital platforms offer instant access to courses and virtual workshops, connecting you to a global community of like-minded explorers. Yet, balance is key. Embrace technology as a complement to traditional practices, not a replacement. It's easy to fall into the digital trap, so set boundaries. Create a digital wellness plan to prevent tech overload, incorporating periodic detoxes to refocus on personal growth. The right blend of tech and tradition can elevate your healing experience to new heights.

Envisioning the Future of Self-Healing Practices

Imagine a future where self-healing integrates with technology, customizing wellness to your needs. AI can tailor healing practices by analysing your unique health patterns. Advances in biofeedback and wearables, e.g. smart watches, could make tracking emotional states as common as tracking steps. This evolution encourages active participation, from contributing to research to sharing your experiences. Envision traditional and alternative health professionals collaborating, embedding self-healing into mainstream care. As acceptance grows, holistic health could become universally accessible. Stay hopeful and engaged, celebrating the progress so far.

Conclusion

Wow, look at you! You've made it to the end of "Self-Healing for Beginners: The First Steps to Better Health." Remember, the main goal of this book was to guide you through the basics of self-healing. Whether it's reducing stress, adopting healthier lifestyle habits, or learning self-preservation, you now have the tools to take charge of your own well-being.

Let's do a quick recap. We started by laying the foundation of self-healing, understanding energy systems like chakras and auras, and how thoughts can affect your health. You learned about breathing exercises for instant calm, progressive muscle relaxation, and other stress-reduction techniques. You also delved into emotional and mental healing practices, learned how to create a personalized self-healing plan, and explored how to build a supportive community.

Key takeaways? Self-awareness is your superpower. Integrating mind, body, and spirit is essential, and consistency in practice is your best friend on this journey. The vision here was to empower you to take control of your health through accessible self-healing practices. I hope you feel that empowerment now.

What's next? Start your self-healing journey today. Apply the techniques you've learned and commit to a daily practice. It's not just about reading; it's about action. Reflect on your growth and consider how you can continue evolving. Reach out and connect with others who are on a similar path. Building a community will enrich your experience.

Obstacles? Sure, they might pop up. But remember, resilience and adaptability are your allies. You've got this! Thank you for trusting me to guide you. Your journey means a lot to me, and I'm grateful to have been a part of it.

Keep that curiosity alive. Continue to explore new modalities and deepen your understanding of holistic wellness. And as you move forward, remember: you've got the power to heal and thrive. Here's to Hope, confidence, and a future of well-being and balance.

Note: names used in this book have been changed to protect confidentiality.

References

- Self-healing forces and concepts of health and disease. A ... https://pub med.ncbi.nlm.nih.gov/11939425/
- *A Beginner's Guide to the 7 Chakras and Their Meanings* https://www.heal thline.com/health/fitness-exercise/7-chakras
- *Psychoneuroimmunology: The Mind-Body Connection* https://blog.bioticsr esearch.com/psychoneuroimmunology-the-mind-body-connection
- *10 Common Misconceptions About Energy Healing* https://discoverhealing. com/articles/10-common-misconceptions-energy-healing/
- *Breathing Practices for Stress and Anxiety Reduction* https://pmc.ncbi.nlm. nih.gov/articles/PMC10741869/
- *What Is Guided Imagery and How Does It Improve Mental ...* https://westco astrecoverycenters.com/blog/what-is-guided-imagery-and-how-does-it-improve-mental-health/
- *Progressive Muscle Relaxation: Benefits, How-To, Technique* https://ww w.healthline.com/health/progressive-muscle-relaxation#:~:text=Prog ressive%20muscle%20relaxation%20(PMR)%20is%20a%20relaxation% 20technique.,pain%20relief%20and%20better%20sleep.
- *Gratitude Journaling and Mental Health* https://recoverycentersofameric a.com/blogs/gratitude-journaling-and-mental-health/
- *Balancing Chakras: Techniques & Practices* https://arohanyoga.com/blog/ balancing-chakras-techniques-practices/
- *Defining Meridians: A Modern Basis of Understanding* https://www.scienc edirect.com/science/article/pii/S2005290110600143
- *Grounding Techniques for Effective Anxiety and Stress Relief* https://www.r esiliencelab.us/thought-lab/grounding-techniques

- *Sound Healing & Aromatherapy: Cleanse Your Space and Aura* https://attun ergy.com/sound-healing-aromatherapy-cleanse-your-space-and-aura/

- *Emotional Release Therapy: 47 Ways To Be Free And ...* https://jeannenangl e.com/31-emotional-release-methods-to-help-you-be-free-and-happy
- *Resilience: Build skills to endure hardship* https://www.mayoclinic.org/tes ts-procedures/resilience-training/in-depth/resilience/art-20046311
- *13 Brain Exercises to Help Keep You Mentally Sharp* https://www.healthlin e.com/health/mental-health/brain-exercises
- *The Power of Positive Affirmations | Old Dominion University* https://ww w.odu.edu/equity/civility-month/affirmations#:~:text=Affirmations% 20are%20positive%20statements%20that,way%20you%20feel%20abou t%20things.
- *Self Assessment Tools | Mandel Wellness Pathway* https://case.edu/medic ine/wellness-pathway/programs/wellness-resources/self-assessment- tools
- *How to Set and Use SMART Goals* https://www.verywellmind.com/smart- goals-for-lifestyle-change-2224097
- *Self-Healing Techniques for a Happier, Healthier Mind* https://www.veryw ellmind.com/self-healing-techniques-8665438
- *Tools to Track Your Wellness Goals* https://www.aao.org/physician-welln ess/goal-tracking-tools
- *Reiki Is Better Than Placebo and Has Broad Potential as a ...* https://pmc.nc bi.nlm.nih.gov/articles/PMC5871310/
- *Energy Medicine: Current Status and Future Perspectives* https://pmc.ncbi. nlm.nih.gov/articles/PMC6396053/
- *Mindfulness Meditation Is Related to Long-Lasting ...* https://pmc.ncbi.nlm. nih.gov/articles/PMC6312586/
- *Client experiences of virtual energy healing - PMC* https://pmc.ncbi.nlm.ni h.gov/articles/PMC10212593/
- *The Role of Community in Emotional Healing: Building a ...* https://mediu m.com/@ladyjewels/the-role-of-community-in-emotional-healing-bu ilding-a-supportive-network-for-emotional-stability-77d173abedcb

- *Understanding the Power of Group Dynamics in Therapy* https://www.grand rising behavioralhealth.com/blog/understanding-the-power-of-group-dynamics-in-therapy
- *How You Can Create a Healing Environment at Home* https://www.takingc harge.csh.umn.edu/how-you-can-create-healing-environment-home
- *Energy Medicine Professional Association: Home* https://www.energymedi cineprofessionalassociation.com/
- *Advanced Chakra Healing - Complete Guide to Your ...* https://www.udem y.com/course/7-chakras-the-complete-guide-to-your-energy-body/
- *The History of Usui Reiki and the Reiki Principles | London* https://www.rei ki-meditation.co.uk/the-history-of-usui-reiki/
- *Healing Crystals 101: Everything You Need to Know* https://www.healthlin e.com/health/mental-health/guide-to-healing-crystals
- *The science and history of sound therapy* https://cambridgesleepsciences.c om/news/the-science-and-history-of-sound-therapy/
- *5 barriers to self care and how to overcome them* https://www.aliciajohnson onlinetherapy.com/blog-1/5-barriers-to-self-care-and-what-you-can-do-to-overcome-them
- *Mastering Time Management through Mindfulness* https://lynnwonders. medium.com/mastering-time-management-through-mindfulness-66d 23defc998
- *Holistic Healing: Nurturing Mind, Body, and Spirit* https://www.news-medical.net/health/Holistic-Healing-Nurturing-Mind-Body-and-Spir it.aspx
- *Five Science-Backed Strategies to Build Resilience* https://greatergood.ber keley.edu/article/item/five_science_backed_strategies_to_build_resili ence
- *The Healing Power of Storytelling | Harvard Medicine Magazine* https://mag azine.hms.harvard.edu/articles/healing-power-storytelling
- *Nurturing Mental Health in the Workplace: A Guide to ...* https://www.li nkedin.com/pulse/nurturing-mental-health-workplace-guide-healing-self-care-mazhar-khan-q1gjf
- *How Self-Healing E-Skin Is Transforming Health Technology* https://www

REFERENCES

.technologynetworks.com/applied-sciences/news/how-self-healing-e-skin-is-transforming-health-technology-396112

- *The Future of Holistic Health: Trends and Innovations to ...* https://www.iphm.co.uk/blog/the-future-of-holistic-health-trends-and-innovations-to-watch-in-2025/

Printed in Dunstable, United Kingdom

77159056R00031